GEORGE H. W. BUSH

OTHER BOOKS BY LOUANN ATKINS TEMPLE IN THE BIOGRAPHY FOR BEGINNING HISTORIANS SERIES

Barbara Bush

George W. Bush

Laura Bush

Lyndon B. Johnson

Lady Bird Johnson

GEORGE H. W. BUSH

A Biography for Beginning Historians

LOUANN ATKINS TEMPLE

THE LBJ FOUNDATION

Distributed by the University of Texas Press

First LBJ Foundation Edition, 2025

♾ The paper used in this book meets the minimum requirements of ANSI/NISO Z39.48-1992 (R1997) (Permanence of Paper).

Library of Congress Control Number: 2025937833

ISBN 978-1-4773-3217-7 (paperback)
ISBN 978-1-4773-3218-4 (PDF)
ISBN 978-1-4773-3219-1 (ePub)

doi:10.7560/332177

To

Allison and Lawrence, my inspiration

CONTENTS

GEORGE H. W. BUSH

INTRODUCTION

You are about to read a book about a lanky, six-foot-two, smiling man, who looked like the baseball player he was; an optimist who knew how to make and keep friends and who practiced loyalty to those he worked for and who worked for him; a dogged competitor who did not gloat in victory and readily shared credit with teammates; a man with wide government experience, who was an insider in the circles of several presidents before he became president himself; a man known for discipline and hard work and modesty but also for adventurousness and playfulness; a man who tended to be awkward in speaking but who penned beautiful, handwritten, fullhearted letters.

Overlaying these personality traits, two principles dictated George Herbert Walker Bush's life: a devotion to duty and a focus on family. These principles guided his decisions as he navigated school, war, marriage, parenthood, career, and retirement. He learned their lessons early, in a family that emphasized both, and they served him and his country well through a long and productive life.

Examples of his service to others abound. When he was in school, he came to the aid of a classmate being taunted by bullies. When he was eighteen, he volunteered to fight in World War II. As a young businessman in Houston, he coached an inner-city baseball team. As president, he and his wife, Barbara, created the Points of Light Foundation to encourage volunteerism in the country. In retirement, he served on the governing board of MD Anderson Cancer Center.

His clearest exposition of the values that guided him is found in a 1991 State of the Union address. He said to Congress and the country:

> We can find meaning and reward by serving some purpose higher than ourselves—a shining purpose, the illumination of a thousand points of light. It is expressed by all who know the irresistible force of a child's hand, of a friend who stands by you and stays there—a volunteer's generous gesture, an idea that is simply right. The problems before us may be different, but the key to solving them remains the same: it is the individual—the individual who steps forward. . . . We all have something to give. So if you know how to read, find someone who can't. If you've got a hammer, find a nail. If you're not hungry, not lonely, not in trouble—seek out someone who is.

Among a thousand points of light, George Bush shone brightly.

CHAPTER 1

GROWING UP IN NEW ENGLAND

George Herbert Walker Bush, the forty-first president of the United States, could claim three distinct areas of the country—New England, Texas, and Washington, DC—as his training grounds. Congressman Jim Wright made this point by introducing him at a dinner for Washington journalists as "the only Texan . . . who eats lobster with his chili."

First, he was a New Englander, born near Boston, in Milton, Massachusetts, on June 12, 1924. His parents, Prescott and Dorothy Walker Bush, named him after his maternal grandfather, George Herbert Walker. They called him Little Pop or Poppy to distinguish him from his namesake, called Pop, and this nickname stuck with him among his family and close friends all his life. Prescott, called Pressy, was the Bushes' first child, two years older than George. A sister, Nancy, and two more brothers, Jonathan and William (nicknamed Bucky), completed the family.

When George was about six months old, the family moved to Greenwich, Connecticut, a town of about thirty thousand people, a thirty-minute train ride from New York City, where George's father had taken a job with a big corporation. In their five-bedroom house, Pressy and Poppy shared a bedroom. When they moved to a larger house with five bedrooms on the second floor and three more on the third, their mother insisted they should have separate rooms, but after a few months, they told her that all they wanted for Christmas that year was to get to room together again, and she conceded. The house lay on two acres off a tree-lined country road. A big porch wrapped around the house, a carriage house stood next to the main house, and a brook ran through the backyard—an idyllic playscape for growing children.

The Bushes were a game-playing family, with a Ping-Pong table set up in the front hall of their house and a tiddlywinks game always on a living room table. On Sundays, they attended services at the Episcopal church, and each day their mother read the Bible to them. Much of their free time was taken up with sports—touch football, baseball, tobogganing in winter, tennis, golf, and more. The family liked to sing, but they teased Poppy that he was the only one who couldn't carry a tune.

Summers at his grandparents' house on the Maine coast at Kennebunkport were active. Surrounded by grandparents, uncles, aunts, and cousins in houses neighboring one another, the family played many competitive games from baseball and golf to footraces and horseshoes, and, always, tennis. It was said that a Bush child was not an adult until he or she beat George's mother in tennis. The family considered Poppy the star athlete among the young people. "He had the fastest eye-hand coordination of any person I have ever known," remembered one participant. George especially liked fishing off his grandfather's lobster boat for mackerel or pollock: "For pure summertime pleasure, bringing one in," he said, "ranked right up there with eating ice cream and staying up late."

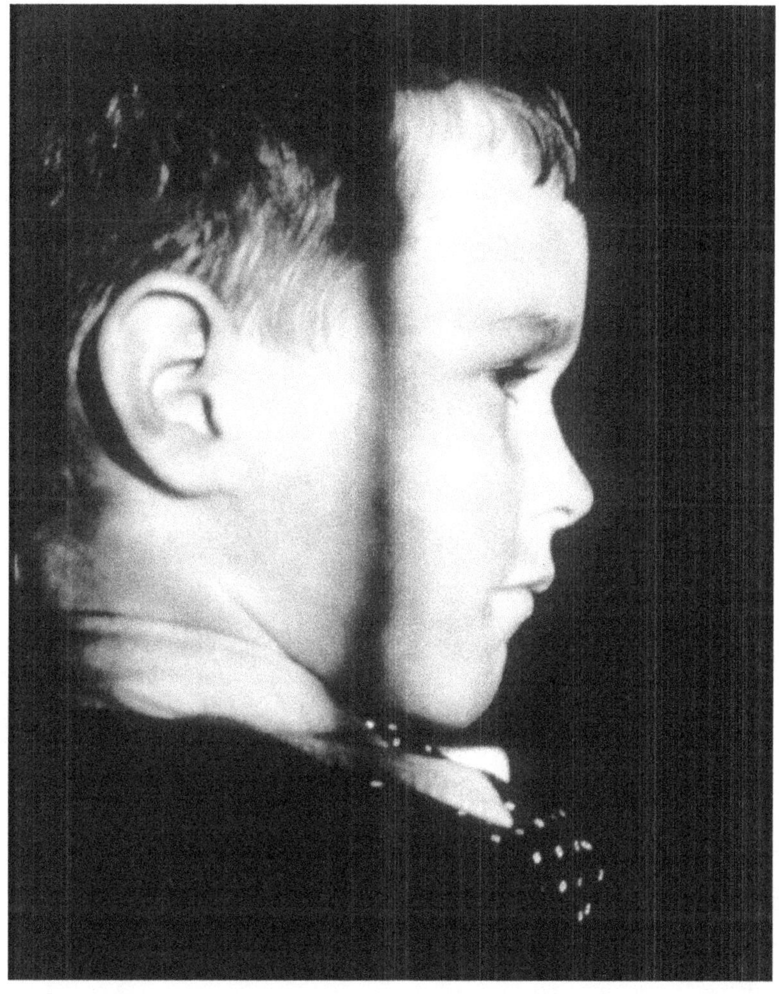

George Herbert Walker Bush at age twelve, 1936. Courtesy of George H. W. Bush Presidential Library and Museum.

George's mother, a small, trim woman, influenced him profoundly. His brother Bucky described her this way: "Mother was very hands-on, quite strict, but in a loving way. . . . If you weren't studying, you better be doing something physical . . . because she didn't like idle hands." She excelled at several sports, but her best was tennis. As a teenager, she had been runner-up for the National Girls' Singles title. Once, she played a tennis match in which she wouldn't give up even though her feet were bleeding; she won. She taught George to be fiercely competitive like she was, but there again, her rules were strict: One must play to win but never be a bad sport, never find excuses when losing, and always be a good teammate. She wanted George to be the best at what he did but never a braggart and always a team player. She would admonish him not to have the "la-dee-dahs"—in other words, not to consider himself more important than others or to claim too much credit for his accomplishments. When he told her once that he had scored three goals in a soccer game, she replied, "That's nice, George, but how did the team do?" She emphasized the importance of modesty by occasionally telling him, "There were too many I's in that sentence." One time a friend said to him, "I wish my mother was like yours." George took pride in that comment and repeated it to his own granddaughter many years later.

George's father, Prescott Bush, an imposing six-foot-four-inch-tall man, played a different role. He presided over breakfast with the children each morning before going off to the city for the day and returned home at night expecting the boys to be dressed in coat and tie for dinner. George idolized his father, whom he described as "big. Strong. Principled. Respected by all who knew him. . . . Wonderful sense of humor. . . . He wasn't cozy like Mother. We felt close to him, but not in the same way. He was more the discipline guy." To some people he seemed stern, and he has been described as having a take-charge attitude. One of George's teachers said about him, "He was an authoritarian. Those kids didn't answer him back, [but] he loved those kids." George's sister remembers, "The boys were more scared of Dad than I was."

Prescott Bush was unswerving in his principles. He once left a meeting because someone told an off-color joke. He had a successful Wall Street career and, after George was grown and gone from home, Prescott went to Washington at age fifty-seven to serve for ten years as a Republican senator from Connecticut, retiring before George entered national politics. *Duty* and *service* were important words in his vocabulary. "He wasn't a power-hungry guy," George said about his father. "It was just leadership." At home he belonged to a singing quartet and played a very good golf game.

When older brother Pressy went to Greenwich Country Day School, Poppy was lonely at home without him, so their parents allowed Poppy to start school a year early. There he stayed until, at the age of thirteen, he followed family tradition by going away to boarding school, attending Phillips Academy in Andover, Massachusetts, where he captained the baseball and soccer teams. He had learned his parents' lessons well: He competed with fervor and still valued the teams' well-being over his own performance. These leadership traits, plus an ability to make and keep friends, made him the president of his class in his senior year.

One Andover student particularly remembers George Bush because one day at school some bullies ordered the young student, who was small, to carry a big chair up some stairs. When George saw the toughies laughing at and ridiculing the boy, he helped him lug the chair to the top of the staircase. After this young man grew up to head a large company and to be a US ambassador, he was still telling the story of his school hero George Bush.

Other schoolmates and faculty remembered Poppy warmly as a leader with an enthusiastic approach to all he did. They called him charming and well liked, with a good sense of humor. No one, however, remembered his ever showing any interest in government or politics. That came later.

George lost one year of schooling at Andover because he contracted a staph infection in his right arm, spent six weeks in Mass General Hospital, where he nearly died, and had a long recovery at home. He was forced to repeat that school year.

In his senior year, he met Barbara Pierce (or Bar, as he called her). At a Christmas dance in Greenwich, he spotted her across the room and was smitten. She was wearing a green-and-red dress. He went home to tell his sister Nancy that he had met a wonderful girl who was beautiful and funny. Barbara went home to sit on the side of her mother's bed and report that she had met the nicest, cutest boy, who was named Poppy Bush. The next night they again were at a dance, this time in her hometown of Rye, New York, near Greenwich. They danced together, and he asked her out the following week. But soon the Christmas vacation ended. Seventeen-year-old George returned to Andover, and sixteen-year-old Barbara returned to her boarding school in South Carolina. All winter they wrote to each other, and in the spring she traveled to Massachusetts to his senior prom. It was her first senior prom and her first kiss, and she stayed up all night long after the dance, telling the girl she was staying with how Poppy Bush was "the greatest living human on the face of the earth."

CHAPTER 2

WAR, MARRIAGE, AND COLLEGE

On December 7, 1941, Japan bombed the US naval base at Pearl Harbor in Hawaii, killing more than two thousand Americans. Within twenty-four hours, the United States had declared war against the Japanese in the Pacific and, a few days later, against Japan's allies, Germany and Italy. America had joined World War II.

George Bush, a senior in high school, yearned to enlist in the military but could not do so legally until he was eighteen. His father begged him to go to college rather than enlist, but George Bush believed that duty called; college could wait. At George's high school graduation, the commencement speaker, the secretary of war, urged the students to complete their education before signing up for the military. Afterward, George's father asked if the speaker had caused George to reconsider his decision, but George said no. For the first time in his life, George saw Prescott Bush cry. On his eighteenth birthday, a few days after graduating from high school, he enlisted in the US Navy and left for Naval Aviation Pre-Flight School, a training program for beginning pilots, in Chapel Hill, North Carolina. His father told him goodbye at Pennsylvania Station in New York City.

Barbara was attending boarding school in Charleston, South Carolina, three hundred miles away from George's training camp. On the way to school that fall, her train stopped in Chapel Hill, and they saw each other for a few hours. From Chapel Hill, George wrote his sister, "I miss [Barbara] more than she knows, Nance. I don't know why but she seems so perfect a girl—beautiful, gentle, a wonderful sense of humor, so much fun, etc. I think of her all the time." He didn't see her again until summer, after her high school graduation, when he had seventeen days leave, and his mother invited Barbara to join the Bush family in Kennebunkport. During those few days spent riding bikes, playing on the beach, competing at tennis, and picnicking, they became semi-secretly engaged: They told their families but not their friends. Then they had to part—Poppy back to the Navy, and Bar to Smith College.

In an accelerated training program, George Bush received his wings in less than a year, three days before his nineteenth birthday, making him the youngest pilot in the US Navy. In the years that followed, he grew up fast as he met life-and-death challenges. He joined Torpedo Squadron 51 aboard the USS *San Jacinto* in the Pacific Ocean. His job: piloting a torpedo bomber, an aircraft he named *Barbara*, on missions against the Japanese.

Barbara lost George's letters to her written during this period, but those to his parents, which his mother saved, describe the thrill and the terror of going out on bombing missions during all kinds of weather, some exceedingly rough; the sadness of losing friends in battle, particularly a friend whose plane had disappeared and who might be a prisoner or hiding on an island if he were alive at all; and the worries of his shipmates who had children at home growing up without their fathers. Mostly, however, the tenor of his letters was cheerful. He told his family about the small pleasures aboard ship, such as receiving mail from home or lying in his bunk, dreaming of Barbara and, perhaps, college. Sometimes, he faltered and thought he wanted, instead, to get a job and forget about college altogether. His father replied that he could not agree with this idea. In one letter, George told his parents that Barbara's dad approved of his and Barbara's plan to get married. "We are going to be the happiest Mr. & Mrs. going," he wrote.

On September 2, 1944, twenty-year-old Lieutenant Junior Grade George Bush and his regular crewmate, radioman John Delaney, set out in their Avenger bomber with George's friend Ted White, who usually did not fly but had asked if he could go along as gunner one time for the experience. They, along with three other bombers and a number of fighter planes—F6F Hellcats—headed for the tiny volcanic island of Chichi Jima, intending to take out its radio tower. For some time, this tower had been intercepting US transmissions and warning Japan of planned American attacks. As they approached the island, they were fired upon. One crewman described the antiaircraft fire as the worst he had seen. As they dove steeply toward their target, descending rapidly, the plane's extreme downward pitch made George feel as if he were standing on his head. Suddenly, at eight thousand feet, they were hit, and the plane caught fire. "There was a jolt," he recalled, "as if a massive fist had crunched into the belly of the plane." Bush continued to dive at a speed of two hundred miles an hour until he could drop his payload, four 500-pound bombs, making damaging hits. Only after completing his mission did he head out to sea, hoping to reach the *San Jacinto* in spite of his faltering plane, but the wings spewed fire, and black smoke filled the cockpit, causing him to choke and gasp. He radioed his crew, whom he could not see, to "hit the silk" and parachute out of the plane, but received no answer from them. He pointed the nose of the plane up to take pressure off the hatch in the back so his crew could get it open, and when he thought they had had time to bail out, he straightened out the plane and bailed out himself, hitting his head on the tail as he fell. Floating through space, supported by a torn parachute, he watched his bomber strike the water. When he hit the ocean, he shook free of his chute, inflated his life preserver, and swam to a life raft, which another Avenger overhead pointed out to him by diving over it. By now he was vomiting from having gulped salt water, and his head was bleeding. Already Japanese gunboats headed toward him from Chichi Jima. Frantically, he hand-paddled out to sea while American fighter planes strafed the Japanese boats. He could see his crewmates nowhere, and when he realized they were gone, he sat in his life raft and sobbed. For the rest of his life, he questioned whether he could have done anything more to save them, and he always found their deaths difficult to talk about.

George floated in the shark-filled water for two hours while fighter planes circled above, dropping medical supplies and transmitting his position to the submarine *Finback* fifteen or twenty miles away. The submarine rushed to the site, surfaced near the exhausted pilot, and pulled him aboard, then submerged again while the American fighter planes continued to fly over.

George Bush as a pilot during World War II, in which he served in the Navy from 1942 to 1945. Courtesy of George H. W. Bush Presidential Library and Museum.

For the next thirty days, George—a "zoomie," as submariners called pilots—adapted to life on the submarine, where he was allowed one shower a week, and he wore only pants and sandals, no shirt. He stood lookout for four hours on and eight hours off. His favorite duty was from midnight until 4 a.m. During those hours, despite the harrowing life aboard a submarine, he still noticed the wonders of nature around him. "I'll never forget the beauty of the Pacific," he said, "the flying fish, the stark wonder of the sea, the waves breaking across the bow." These refreshing times alternated with deadly ones when the enemy attacked. He thought being underwater with bombs and depth charges coming at the ship was more frightening than being under fire while on a plane. But despite the challenges aboard the submarine, George maintained his spirits and those of his fellow passengers. One submariner remembers that "he was always saying something to make us laugh. He kept up our morale."

Finally, the submarine let Bush off at Midway, and he was sent to Hawaii for leave. However, he stayed only a few days because he was intent on getting back to the *San Jacinto* in spite of the fact that the Navy gave him the option of returning to duty on the mainland.

Back aboard his own ship, the crew greeted him with a big cake featuring the words *Your First Ducking* on top. Later, the Navy awarded him the Distinguished Flying Cross "for heroism and extraordinary achievement . . . in action against enemy Japanese forces."

Even after so terrifying an experience, George flew eight more missions—fifty-eight in all, including 126 carrier landings and 1,228 total flight hours. Of his squadron's original sixteen pilots, half died in combat. In December of that year,

1944, he was returned to Norfolk, Virginia, where he trained new pilots, and in September of 1945, after the Japanese surrender, he was discharged. He called those three years in the Navy "the most maturing in my life."

When George had joined the Navy, Barbara was still in high school. She graduated around the same time that he received his wings. She attended Smith College for a year and a half while he was overseas. She tried, with little success, to think about her schoolwork. Instead, she read his letters, listened to the war news on the radio (this was before television), wondered where he was, and dreamed of a wedding. Mail delivery was erratic. Some days she received a stack of letters, and then a month would pass without her hearing a word. In September 1944, she received no letters from him until one arrived from a pilot in George's squadron saying that George's plane had been shot down and that from the air he had last seen George swimming toward a raft.

Three dreadful days dragged by before the Bush family heard from the Navy that George was safe on a submarine. He did return to New York a few months later, on Christmas Eve, and just two weeks later he and Barbara married in the First Presbyterian Church in Rye, New York, and honeymooned at the Cloister hotel on Sea Island, Georgia. He was only twenty and she nineteen, and college lay ahead of him. Barbara said in explanation of their young age and unfinished education when they married, "In wartime, the rules change. You don't wait until tomorrow to do anything." (Forty-four years later, Smith College would award First Lady Barbara Bush an honorary degree.)

The war ended seven months later, and all America was giddy with happiness, but none more so than the newly mar-

Barbara and George Bush on their honeymoon on Sea Island, Georgia, January 1945. Courtesy of George H. W. Bush Presidential Library and Museum.

ried Barbara and George Bush. Now they could quit dreading his return to overseas duty and think about their future. The day the armistice was declared, they went to church to thank God and to say a prayer for the many friends they had lost in the war.

One month after the end of World War II, George entered Yale University, the fourth generation of his family to do so. Here, as at Andover and in the Navy, he threw himself into the experience competitively and wholeheartedly and had an easy way with people. School seemed less of a challenge to him after combat duty. He graduated with a degree in economics in two and a half years, a period that was crowded with both academic and athletic achievement as well as the beginning of a family. He not only made Phi Beta Kappa but also captained the baseball team to two Eastern Championships and played in the first College World Series. At one time, pro scouts took a look at this left-handed first baseman. They ultimately determined that he was a strong fielder but a weak hitter. Barbara chose having a family over returning to college, and in the summer after George's first year at Yale, they became the parents of George Walker Bush, another future US president.

Married couples with families were not rare at Yale because so many young men had delayed their educations until after the war. Colleges all over the country burgeoned with huge classes of older, married students. In appreciation of their service to their country, the US government helped pay the tuition and living expenses of veterans through the GI Bill. This group constituted 60 percent of George's class.

CHAPTER 3

MOVING TO TEXAS

George graduated in 1948. At just twenty-four years old, he had proved himself to be a leader, a team player, and a friend at school, in war, and on the athletic field. He had married and started a family, and he was ready for a career. He rejected the offer to go to New York with his father's investment firm and interviewed for many varied jobs, even considering farming (for which he did not have the necessary start-up capital). He knew two things: He must like his job, and he wanted to deal with a real product, not just money. He decided his best opportunity was knocking two thousand miles away in Odessa, Texas, where a family friend offered him a job as a trainee in a company that made equipment for the oil and gas industry.

George and Barbara Bush left their close-knit families and the rooted, self-confident East Coast in their new red Studebaker (a graduation gift from George's family) and headed for West Texas, where wind, sand, cacti, and jackrabbits abounded, big financial deals were finalized with no more than a handshake, and ambitions soared as high as the Texas sky. Although New England had shaped them, George and Barbara took Texas to heart, and George's friendly, open,

I-can-do-it ways made Texans take him to heart also. He and the state were a good fit.

As a trainee, George worked seven-day weeks at menial jobs, such as sweeping out the warehouse and painting oil field equipment (sometimes in 105-degree weather). For a brief time, his company transferred them to California, where their second child, daughter Robin, was born, and then sent him to Midland, Texas, a little more than twenty miles from Odessa. By this time, George had been promoted to salesman. Soon, he quit his job, acquired financing from a family friend back east, and partnered with a neighbor to form Bush-Overbey Oil Development Company, buying drilling rights for customers.

Not long after that, Bush-Overbey joined in partnership with their friends Hugh and Bill Liedtke from Oklahoma to form the Zapata Petroleum Corporation, which drilled wells on a contract basis for major distributors. It was 1953, and growing numbers of young men from across the country were flocking to Texas to participate in the oil boom. In Midland alone, 363 oil companies were doing business, with over two hundred of them having arrived in the area in the past five years. By the end of the decade, this would be the leading oil-producing area in the United States.

Barbara said that life in Midland at this time seemed almost too good to be true. They had Georgie and Robin, and in early 1953 son Jeb was born. They bought their first house. They had cookouts with other families on weekends, and George played touch football with the men. He began to take an interest in politics, running the first Republican primary ever held in Midland. At that time the Republican Party was almost nonexistent in Texas, and only a few people showed up to vote in the Midland primary. Both George and Barbara were active in the theater, were involved with the YMCA, volunteered at the hospital, and taught Sunday school. Then, their life took a tragic turn.

When Jeb was just a few weeks old, they noticed that three-year-old Robin had no energy. A visit and tests at the doctor's office revealed that she had leukemia, a disease that, at that time, had no cure and that the doctor thought would take her life in only a few weeks' time. The very next morning, George and Barbara flew with Robin to New York to see if the doctors at Memorial Sloan Kettering Cancer Center could perhaps prolong her life until a medical breakthrough could save her. But it wasn't to be. Robin died a few months later. During those months, their family and friends cared for the Bushes as best they could. They gave blood. They looked after seven-year-old Georgie and baby Jeb back in Texas. One friend gave them a collie puppy in the hope of bringing some measure of joy into their days. Another friend prayed with George at six thirty every morning at church, and a bachelor friend went to the hospital every day and waited to see if he could be of help.

Several years after Robin's death, eldest son George wrote about his sister, "[Robin] is still with us. We need her and yet we have her. We can't touch her, and yet we feel her. We hope she'll stay in our house for a long, long time."

By the end of the '50s, the oil business had made the Bushes millionaires. George and his partners split Zapata Petroleum into two companies, and thirty-five-year-old George went out on his own as president and CEO of Zapata Off-Shore, which operated offshore drilling equipment in the Gulf of Mexico. With some sadness, the family left Midland, which Barbara called "this cocoon of warmth and love," and moved almost five hundred miles southeast to Houston with their children, now numbering four—George, Jeb, Neil, and Marvin. Soon, their last child, Dorothy (Doro), would be born in Houston.

They built a house. George worked long hours and traveled frequently. When he was in Houston, he liked to play tennis with a new friend, James Baker, who would later be his secretary of state when George became president. Barbara oversaw the activities of four boys and a baby girl. Young George left for school at Phillips Academy in Andover, Massachusetts. Occasionally, George (whose friends still called him Poppy) and Barbara went to New York to go to the theater, to see baseball games, and to visit family. They spent each August at Kennebunkport.

Now that he was financially secure, George became restless to contribute to his community in addition to developing his new business. His father, Prescott Bush, had been elected to the US Senate from Connecticut a few years earlier, after he had built his financial base, and George followed his example of turning to political life after success in business. By this time, the Republican Party in Texas was beginning to be a force to be reckoned with. George ran for chairman of the Harris County Republicans, campaigning in every one of its 270 precincts. He was chosen when his opponent withdrew from the race. He spent the next year building the Republican organization in the Houston area.

Then it looked as if another opportunity was opening for him. Republicans were gaining strength in Texas, and they chose him to challenge Democratic US Senator Ralph Yarborough for his seat in Washington. To campaign, George and Barbara, with young George, who had just graduated from high school, traveled the state in a bus with a country and western band called the Black Mountain Valley Boys. At that time, in most of the counties he visited, no Republican organization existed to help him, so the band would begin playing off the back of a flatbed truck, and George would make a speech to whoever showed up. When he was not speaking, he was handwriting hundreds of thank-you letters to those who made campaign posters or came to hear him speak. "Campaigning in Texas on a statewide basis," he said, "is the most exhausting thing I have ever done." Although he won the largest Republican vote in Texas history, it was not enough to beat Yarborough, especially since another Texan, President Lyndon Johnson, headed the Democratic ticket. Johnson won the presidency in a landslide and carried Yarborough into office with him.

The campaign taught George a valuable lesson. Sometimes, in the heat of political debate, he had taken positions he thought would elect him rather than saying what he believed. He was disappointed in himself and told the pastor at his church that he would not do that again. As a result, Barbara could say about her husband, years later, "I was always proud that George thought each problem out separately and did not take a party line."

In spite of the pain of losing, George Bush knew that political life was for him, and two years later he tried again, for a new congressional seat that had opened up in Houston. This time, he had name recognition and experience campaigning and, instead of trying to continue to run his business along with a campaign, he made what he called an "agonizing decision" to resign as president of Zapata Off-Shore and even to sell his Zapata stock. Zapata Off-Shore had become a public company listed on the American Stock Exchange, with 2,200 stockholders and 195 employees, and was simply too big for him to manage part-time. He chose politics.

This election he won handily, and a new life opened for him and his family. Eighteen years in Texas and in the oil business had ended. It would be over twenty-six years before the Bushes lived in Houston again. Little did George know that in that time, he would win and lose elections and be appointed to widely varying government positions—from congressman, to ambassador to the UN, to chairman of the Republican National Committee, to envoy to China, to head of the Central Intelligence Agency, to vice president, to president. Who could have dreamed such a future?

CHAPTER 4

FROM WASHINGTON, DC, TO NEW YORK TO CHINA AND BACK AGAIN

From staid New England to flamboyant Texas, the Bush family now moved to Washington, DC, the city of protocol, where seniority determined a politician's status, women left calling cards when they visited, and one had to learn how to properly address a Supreme Court justice or a president. Sons George and Jeb were away at school at Yale and at Andover. Barbara stayed in Houston to pack, and George, Neil, Marvin, and Doro went ahead to Washington.

When they first arrived, seven-year-old Doro had heard that Washington girls wore knee socks to school, unlike the short socks she had worn in Houston. She dreaded the first day of school, afraid she would show up wearing the wrong socks. Her father solved the problem by going across the street from their new house, introducing himself to the child who lived there, and asking her what kind of socks Doro should wear. This same child remembered that when her own father died a few years later, George Bush was the only adult who wrote her a letter of sympathy. She would save that letter for the rest of her life.

During the day, George studied such serious issues facing the country as the war in Vietnam and civil rights and kept in contact with his district through letters, phone calls, and speeches, often traveling back and forth to Houston, while Barbara met other congressional wives at numerous luncheons and coffees and showed the sites of the capital to constituents from home. At night they attended what Barbara called "unending" receptions and black-tie dinners. They tried to reserve Sundays for church and lunch with just their family and friends, a time George described as their "oasis of privacy."

George received two honors during his first year as a congressman. His colleagues, responding to his friendly personality, as people had done all his life, elected him president of their freshman class, and his party chose him for the powerful House Ways and Means Committee (the chief tax-writing committee). He was the first freshman congressman to be a member of that committee in sixty-three years.

George Bush soon had an opportunity to put to the test his promise to his pastor that he would vote his conscience and not bow to the pressure to gain popularity among voters. In 1968, Black and white people lived in almost entirely racially segregated communities. Then, President Johnson introduced a civil rights bill—supported by Congressman Bush—called the Fair Housing Act, which stated that a person who wanted to buy a house could not be refused because of their race. The idea of a big change in their neighborhoods frightened many people because the races had always lived separately from one another, and they didn't know what living together would be like. Some of Bush's main money backers were angry with him, and most of his mail and telephone calls strongly opposed the Fair Housing Act. Some even threatened him with death, but he believed that all races could and should live peacefully together, so he voted for the bill. After the bill passed, he went to a public meeting in Houston to explain his vote. The crowd booed him when he stood up to talk. He spoke his heart to those four hundred people, reminding them that Black Americans were fighting for them in Vietnam. "Somehow it seems fundamental," he said, "that a man . . . should not have a door slammed in his face if he is a Negro or speaks with a Latin American accent." When he finished, the audience stood and cheered him. America was changing, and he was helping it to do so. When he ran for Congress again, he was unopposed.

In 1968, when Richard Nixon became the Republican candidate for president, he considered asking George Bush to be his vice presidential running mate but, in the end, chose the governor of Maryland, Spiro Agnew, instead. Bush, although disappointed, campaigned for them. On the day of Nixon's inauguration, George was thinking of the departing president, Lyndon Johnson, as well as the incoming one, Richard Nixon. Rather than stay in town to celebrate with elated Republicans, he drove to the airport to pay honor to former President Johnson, a Democrat, as he ended his thirty-one-year career in Washington and returned to Texas. Bush was the only Republican congressman from Texas there. The Johnsons deeply appreciated the gesture, and Lady Bird Johnson remembered later, "Through the years, I have been the recipient of so many generous messages of love, support, and encouragement from George Bush—mostly handwritten! But

Congressman George Bush (*center left*) with his family (*left to right:* Jeb, Marvin, Doro, Barbara, Neil, and George W.) in front of the United States Capitol, Washington, DC, 1967. Bush served as a congressman from Texas from 1967 to 1971. Courtesy of George H. W. Bush Presidential Library and Museum.

engraved on my heart is a cold January 20 in 1969 when Lyndon and I said our farewell to Washington and departed for Texas. There in the crowd at Andrews Air Force Base was George Bush. . . . George Bush is not only a strong Republican but he is a very warm and caring man who wrote the book on friendship!"

Four years into his congressional career, George decided to try again for the Senate. After having run his own business, he disliked being a junior member of a minority party in which he had little chance of making things happen. He thought this time he could win against his old opponent Ralph Yarborough because the state as a whole was more conservative than Yarborough. The Democrats, however, surprised him by choosing centrist Lloyd Bentsen instead of the liberal Yarborough as their candidate. Bentsen and Bush differed little on their positions. Conservative Texas still tended to vote Democratic, and once again George Bush lost. It would be ten years before he won another election, this time as vice president. The night of the Senate election, Doro sobbed, saying, "I'm the only person in the fifth grade whose dad doesn't have a job." George, meanwhile, worried about his staff members who were now out of jobs also. The day after the election, instead of staying home and licking his wounds, he got on the phone, trying to help them find new work.

He did not remain jobless for long. President Richard Nixon soon asked him to represent the United States at the United Nations, an organization of 127 countries (193 by 2025) meeting together to discuss their mutual problems. The Bush family moved into the forty-second floor of the Waldorf-Astoria Hotel in New York, near UN headquarters.

All the Bush boys had moved out, and only twelve-year-old Doro moved with them. This job served George Bush well because he made friends with other representatives from around the world with whom he would work again when he became president and they had become governmental leaders in their countries.

Diplomats transacted their work, not only at official meetings during the day, but after hours at parties, which suited George, since he enjoyed entertaining. Many parties were formal, but he particularly liked to invite his guests to do something out of the ordinary, like attend a Texas barbecue or a professional baseball game—he and Barbara found that explaining the game of baseball to foreigners could be almost impossible. Sometimes, they'd even take guests to a Sunday lunch in Connecticut at George's parents' house.

Sixth grader Doro moved to New York reluctantly, but she soon discovered the fun of riding up and down in the hotel's elevators and seeing celebrities in the lobby. Each morning her father's limousine dropped her off at the United Nations School attended by diplomats' children. Showing up at school in a limousine embarrassed her, so her father asked the driver to take them in a sedan. Doro later realized that she had been too self-conscious to notice that many diplomats' children also arrived at school in limousines.

One afternoon, one of Doro's friends was visiting the Bushes' apartment. The girls looked out the window of the U-shaped building to see, on the other side of the U, one floor down, a naked man lying on a bed. The girls got the giggles at this unlikely sight and made a poster saying, "Hi there," which they dropped out the window by a string in front of the man's window. Immediately, a woman in his room closed the curtains, and the two girls laughed until they cried. When they confessed to Doro's father what they had done, Ambassador Bush said sternly, "Do you realize that everyone knows the US ambassador to the United Nations lives on the forty-second floor?" but the girls knew he was trying to keep from laughing too.

In the family's two years in New York, Barbara volunteered every week at Memorial Sloan Kettering, the hospital where their daughter Robin had died twenty years earlier. She had to explain her work to her foreign friends at the UN from countries where volunteerism was not common. During this period, George's father became a patient in the same hospital, and George visited very often. George's father died within a month, and he was buried next to Robin in Greenwich, Connecticut, where George had grown up. George and Barbara were thankful that they had lived so close to his father in his last year of life.

President Nixon had other plans for George Bush only two years after appointing him to the UN. He asked Bush to become chairman of the national Republican Party. George disliked leaving the world of international affairs that he loved and being thrust back into partisan politics, but loyalty demanded that he not turn the president down, and the challenge of growing the Republican Party appealed to him. Especially, he wanted to win over young people, whom he feared were becoming cynical about the government. Barbara, George, and Doro moved back to Washington.

George arrived at Republican headquarters in early 1973, not long after Nixon had won reelection and not long before the scandal of Watergate began unfolding in newspapers and on television, making George's job as Republican national chairman immensely more difficult. The Watergate story had begun during the campaign the year before, when police had arrested five men in the process of breaking into Democratic National Committee headquarters in the Watergate Building in Washington while attempting to wiretap offices and steal secret documents. The burglars turned out to be connected to President Nixon's reelection campaign, but people in the president's office succeeded for months in keeping the public from knowing that the burglary had even taken place. It was never determined that Nixon knew about the break-in before it happened, but when the cover-up by his office became known, the publicity damaged Nixon and the Republican Party in the public's eye. Before the investigation was finished, almost fifty people went to jail as a result of the uncovering of many other dirty political tricks, and Nixon resigned from office rather than face possible impeachment proceedings. (Impeachment is the introduction of a formal document in the House of Representatives that charges a public official with misconduct in office. If a president is impeached by the House, he goes to trial before the Senate, which can remove him from office.)

On August 7, 1974, George Bush delivered a letter to Nixon's office, which began, "Dear Mr. President, It is my considered judgment that you should now resign." Bush did not come to this belief easily, but he knew from his job traveling the country to help Republican officeholders how ruinous the Watergate story was. Doro wrote of this period, "My father was under enormous strain. Leading a political party whose president was sinking deeper and deeper into a legal, political, and ethical quagmire with each passing day must have been more than most people could have endured." At noon on August 9, 1974, two days after George had delivered his letter, President Nixon resigned, and Vice President Gerald R. Ford became president. George and Barbara Bush waved goodbye to the Nixons on the White House lawn as they flew away in a helicopter, then turned and went inside to witness the swearing-in of the new president. Barbara Bush wrote later about how great America is in its ability to transition "gently and quickly" from one president to another.

In the midst of this turmoil, friends had encouraged George to run for governor of Texas, but he felt that he should stay in the Republican chairmanship to help his party through its difficult time, even though, as he wrote to his boys, "I feel battered and disillusioned." A happier event during this period was twenty-one-year-old Jeb's wedding in Austin, where he was a student at the University of Texas.

Soon, President Ford offered George Bush an ambassadorship. The president suggested London or Paris, but, still loving adventure as he had when he moved to Texas, Bush chose to be an envoy to China. That home of a billion people—one of the oldest civilizations on Earth, virtually unknown to Americans, and destined to be a big player on the world's stage—was a mystery waiting to be solved. Even though China was halfway across the world, Barbara was delighted that she and George would now be together most of the time instead of his frequently having to travel the country on business as his job as Republican chairman had demanded. The time away from American politics would allow him a chance to refresh himself after the exhausting experience of the past several months.

In the fall of 1974, Barbara and George and their blond cocker spaniel C. Fred moved to Beijing. (Many Chinese people had never seen that breed of dog and thought he was a kind of cat.) The two oldest Bush children were grown and gone from home, and the three youngest were attending boarding schools in the United States.

Within an hour of their arriving, after a seven-thousand-mile trip, the Bushes held a party for the office staff of fifty-three Americans.

Immense cultural differences awaited the Bushes. The household staff spoke no English. Banks made calculations on abaci. Dishes served at dinner parties included slugs and, one time, the upper lip of a wild dog. Bicycles were a common form of transportation. In the countryside, carts were pulled by camels, donkeys, or people, and sometimes a bicycle rider appeared with a wiggling pig tied to his side. The Chinese sped through the streets with one hand on the horn, one foot on the brake, and no headlights.

In the summertime, sunflowers seemed to be growing in every empty spot in the city. In the fall, the flower heads were cut off and put on rooftops to dry and the seeds made into oil. Cabbages, too, dried on the roofs, to be eaten during the winter. Harsh winds brought such bad dust storms that C. Fred turned gray and had to be bathed often because he slept in the bed with the Bushes.

The Christian church that the Bushes attended conducted services in Chinese, and everyone sang the hymns in their own language.

George and Barbara saw their job as one of making American and Chinese people better friends and set about getting to know the locals, a difficult task because Chinese citizens tended to keep to themselves. The Bushes felt certain the Chinese government spied on them in their own house, so Barbara gave up writing in her diary until they returned home.

As always, they entertained frequently. They also bicycled and played tennis and explored the Great Wall of China, the Forbidden City, and the Chinese opera. George immersed himself in Chinese history, and he and Barbara took a class in that difficult language five days a week just before lunch.

Barely a year after the Bushes arrived in China, President Ford shocked them when he asked George to come home and head up the Central Intelligence Agency (CIA), whose job was to gather information about foreign governments and individuals who might want to harm the United States. In other words, George would run a spy agency. He knew he would be facing problems as explosive as he had as Republican national chairman, and he knew that no one had ever moved from the CIA to any high elected office. It was an unlikely stepping stone. He wrote his siblings, "It is perhaps the toughest job in government right now. . . . It is my duty and I'll do it."

The CIA was under criticism by people who feared that it was doing illegal things overseas and spying on its own citizens, and some questioned how much and how wisely the agency was spending money. As a result, morale among employees was low. George dealt with these problems in addition to performing his main duty—keeping America safe.

During George's tenure with the agency, CIA employees gained his great respect. Barbara said he thought they were the most dedicated and the brightest in the government. "People who serve," he said, "never sit at the head table or get recognition, and are serving for the right patriotic reasons—belief in service to country." More than twenty years later,

George Bush as CIA director, a position he held from 1976 to 1977. Courtesy of George H. W. Bush Presidential Library and Museum.

the CIA building was named the George Bush Center for Intelligence.

Once again, George's job—which he told a friend was the most interesting one he had ever had—lasted only a year. Democratic Governor Jimmy Carter defeated President Ford in the presidential election, and President Carter wanted his own appointee in the position of director of intelligence at the CIA.

George and Barbara returned home to Houston, Texas, to figure out the next step in their lives. It looked as if fifty-two-year-old George Bush's career in politics had come to an end.

He tried to interest himself in business opportunities, but being away from the action in Washington left him bored and restless. Before long he asked his friend James Baker to help him explore the possibility of running for president. They traveled the country to meet people and make George Bush known. In 1978 alone, Bush visited forty-two of the fifty states. Then, in 1979, he formally announced his candidacy for the 1980 election. In a crowded field of competitors, polls showed that only a small margin of voters favored him, but he began to gain what he called the Big Mo (a sports term meaning "big momentum"), and by virtue of tireless person-to-person campaigning, he drew ahead as one of the front-runners alongside Ronald Reagan, a former movie star and governor of California. These two traded primary wins back and forth until it became obvious that Reagan would be the Republican choice.

Bush reluctantly withdrew from the race. With a light touch to mask his disappointment, he announced his decision to staff and reporters on his campaign plane by playing over the loudspeaker Kenny Rogers's hit song "The Gambler," which featured these words: "You've got to know when to hold 'em, know when to fold 'em / Know when to walk away, know when to run."

The joy of the campaign had been in its being a family affair. Besides Barbara, George W. (now in the oil business in Midland, as his father had been nearly thirty years before) hit the campaign trail; Jeb and his wife, Columba, came home from Venezuela, where he was working in a bank so that he could travel with his father; Marvin, Neil (who would get married during the campaign), and Doro all took off from school to help out; and a number of uncles, aunts, cousins, nieces, and nephews worked the country.

When campaign money ran low, some employees expressed their loyalty by continuing without pay. After the campaign was over, Bush held fundraisers to reimburse them for their unpaid salaries.

After this latest defeat, Bush said to a friend, "No one died but it feels like it." Heavyhearted, the Bushes attended the Republican National Convention in Detroit, where Bush gave a speech endorsing Ronald Reagan, who was named the party's candidate. The couple then returned to their hotel room to pack and go back to Houston and an uncertain future. The telephone rang at 11 p.m. "Hello, this is Ron Reagan," said the familiar voice on the other end of the line. "I've been thinking about it, and I wonder if you would be willing to be my vice presidential candidate."

Almost immediately the Secret Service appeared to protect the new candidate. The next morning the Bushes and Reagans met for breakfast to get to know each other better, and the campaign began against President Jimmy Carter and his running mate, Vice President Walter Mondale.

Vice President Bush and President Ronald Reagan, February 1981. Bush served as Reagan's vice president from 1981 to 1989. Courtesy of George H. W. Bush Presidential Library and Museum.

In November, voters named Ronald Reagan the fortieth president of the United States, with George Bush, thirteen years younger, as his vice president. Barbara remembered that day. "I still couldn't believe it. We had worked so hard—yet it seemed so sudden. In May, we had bowed out of politics forever; six months later, I was the wife of the vice president-elect."

In typical kindly fashion, Bush's first action was to handwrite thank-you notes. One of the letters was written to Vice President Mondale, whom he had defeated. It said, "I'd love to sit down with you. Thank you for your wire, your call, your just plain decency. I've lost plenty—I know—it's no fun." He had lost a few races: Twice he had run unsuccessfully for Senate, once he had run for the Republican presidential nomination, and he had been considered as a possible vice presidential candidate by Richard Nixon and by Gerald Ford before they each chose someone else. With persistence, he finally had won.

The vice president's primary job is to take over for the president should the president be incapacitated. That is exactly what happened a little more than two months after Reagan took office. He was leaving the Hilton hotel in Washington, where he had just made a speech, when twenty-five-year-old John Hinckley Jr., waiting on the street, shot at him six times, injuring the president, his press secretary, a Secret Service agent, and a policeman. Hinckley was arrested at the scene, the president was rushed to the hospital, and Vice President Bush, on a trip to Texas, was notified. Within four and a half hours of the shooting, Bush was on duty in the White House, making it clear to the world and the American people that the government would continue to function in spite of anyone's attempts to disrupt it.

When President Reagan recovered and returned to his office, he and Vice President Bush met together for lunch every Thursday to discuss the nation's problems. Bush quickly learned that President Reagan loved a good joke, and every week the vice president made sure he had one to tell the president. He wanted to lighten the president's load in small ways as well as big.

Frequently, George Bush represented the president at meetings and funerals in foreign countries. In eight years, he visited sixty-two countries. Dealing with other nations was his favorite part of his job.

CHAPTER 5

THE PRESIDENCY

In 1984 the Reagan–Bush team was reelected to the second of the two four-year terms the Constitution allows a president. Then, in 1987, as Reagan was leaving office, George Bush announced once again his own candidacy for the job. He won the nomination of his party, and in his acceptance speech at the Republican National Convention in New Orleans, he made a statement that would come back to haunt him. "My opponent won't rule out raising taxes," he said. "But I will. And the Congress will push me to raise taxes and I'll say no. And they'll push, and I'll say no." Here he put his finger to his mouth and continued. "And they'll push again, and I'll say to them: 'Read my lips: no new taxes!'" The audience cheered, and newscasts repeated the pledge over and over, and this statement aided him in a November victory over his Democratic opponent, Governor Michael Dukakis of Massachusetts.

Bush chose Senator Dan Quayle of Indiana as his running mate, and Dukakis ran with Senator Lloyd Bentsen of Texas, the man who had, eighteen years earlier, defeated Bush for a Senate seat from Texas. This time Bush won. In twenty-two years he had worked his way from congressman to ambassador to the United Nations to chairman of the Republican Party to US liaison to China to director of the Central Intelligence Agency to vice president, and now he held the most important job in the country. He was president of the United States.

His children, who were all married, and ten grandchildren, some in their parents' arms, arrived in Washington for the inauguration, which spilled over with events from early in the morning until late at night. That bitterly cold January day—the two hundredth anniversary of the presidency—began with a prayer service at St. John's Episcopal Church, just across from the White House, followed by coffee at the White House with outgoing President and Mrs. Reagan. Barbara held the Bible as Bush rested his hand on it to take the oath of office on the steps of the Capitol. After lunch in the Capitol rotunda, the Bushes rode in a limousine back to the White House. The new President and Mrs. Bush jumped out of the car repeatedly to shake hands and wave at the crowds lining the streets. Then followed a parade, which they watched from a glass-enclosed viewing stand in front of the White House. Seventy-eight floats passed by, including one that held the surviving members of Bush's old Navy squadron of forty-five years ago. That night they fell into bed exhausted after dancing at fourteen different balls. Later, they had a prayer service at the National Cathedral, then lunch at the White House with 250 family members. Finally, the festivities ended, President Bush walked into the Oval Office, placed his beloved Robin's picture on his desk, and went to work.

President Bush particularly liked dealing with other countries. He had forged friendships all over the world and garnered experience in foreign affairs during his work at the United Nations, in China, and as vice president.

Immediately after being sworn in as president, he telephoned nearly two dozen foreign leaders just to get to know them better. Some of the surprised heads of state had not had the experience of being called by the president of the United States before and even thought they might be receiving a prank call. Bush continued this practice throughout his presidency.

His first appointment was of his friend, tennis partner, and campaign manager, James Baker, as secretary of state, the person who assists the president in foreign affairs.

He would also have to use his foreign affairs expertise in dealing with the Soviet Union (USSR). For more than forty years, since the end of World War II, America and the USSR had fought the Cold War, a war not of guns but of propaganda. The two nations vied with each other to win world opinion as to which had the better political system: democracy or communism. Each built its weapons supply to show the world how strong it was; each tried to be the first to conquer space to illustrate its predominance in science and technology; and each supported smaller countries who were fighting political wars.

By the time George Bush took office, Mikhail Gorbachev had been the leader of the USSR for four years. With the nation's struggling economy and its satellite countries resentful of the oppressive rule and corruption of the Soviet government, Gorbachev knew that the USSR must be revitalized. He believed that could be achieved by having more contact with the West, by spending money on priorities more important than nuclear weapons, and by allowing voices other than Communists to be heard within the country. This was good news for the United States, but Bush first wanted to be sure that Gorbachev meant what he said and could be trusted to deal fairly with the West. He invited the Soviet leader to meet with him—just the two of them, with no agenda and without the press or many staffers around—"to reduce the chances there could be any misunderstanding between us" and "to get our relationship on a more personal basis," as he said in a letter to Gorbachev.

In 1961, the Soviet Union, denying those under its control access to their Western neighbors, had built a concrete wall between Communist East Berlin and democratic West Berlin and would not allow East Berliners to cross the wall to visit their fellow Germans. Guards were ordered to shoot anyone trying to escape over the wall. People referred to the real barriers, such as the Berlin Wall, and the ideological barriers, such as those between the Communist and the democratic political systems, as the Iron Curtain.

The first year Bush was in office, Gorbachev allowed the Berlin Wall to be opened, and more than twenty thousand elated East Germans crossed into West Germany in the first hour. For days and weeks they laughed and cried and cheered in celebration and chipped away at the wall with sledgehammers to take souvenirs. Finally, the government brought in big machinery to demolish the wall entirely.

Many in the press and the public criticized President Bush for quietly accepting this monumental change without proclaiming to the world that democracy had won. Some thought he should fly to Germany and stand on the breached Berlin Wall, waving an American flag in triumph. Bush, however, did not believe in ideological one-upmanship. He

President Bush meets with reporters after the fall of the Berlin Wall, November 1989. Courtesy of George H. W. Bush Presidential Library and Museum.

knew how fragile the changes occurring in Eastern Europe were and that the Soviet Union might well reverse some of its tentative moves toward a more open society if the Americans took credit for pushing them into change. The Soviet Union did not want to look weak to the rest of the world. What the public did not know was that Gorbachev had called President Bush and asked him not to gloat because that might make those in the Soviet Union who disagreed with Gorbachev try to push him out of office.

The two countries still needed to talk about reducing their military arms and their nuclear arsenals for the safety of the world and discuss how to strengthen their relations. President Bush and Secretary Gorbachev met three times in the next two years, once for four hours on a ship off the coast of Malta, once for a weekend at the White House, and once in Moscow. They talked frankly with each other about the dangers inherent in their two countries' competition, especially their fears of an accidental nuclear war. Bush spoke firmly about his democratic beliefs and objections to Soviet aggression against its neighboring countries, and he listened carefully as Gorbachev described his own concerns. He felt as if Gorbachev displayed the same forthrightness with him.

At one point, Bush expressed, in personal terms, how strongly he felt about the need for cooperation. He wrote a letter to Gorbachev saying that on Thanksgiving Day, "I will give thanks that you are pressing forward with *glasnost-perestroika* [the Russian words for "openness" and "reform"], for you see, the fate of my own precious grandkids and yours depends on *perestroika*'s success." During his tenure, the United States and the Soviet Union signed an arms-reduction agreement, and each decreased its nuclear arsenal. President Bush's quiet, undramatic diplomacy, for which he was so criticized, paid off by ensuring a safer world.

At the end of 1991, Gorbachev signed a law dissolving the Soviet Union, leading to the emergence of fifteen independent countries, including Russia, which remained the biggest and most powerful. The Iron Curtain had fallen, and the Cold War, which had divided the East and West and caused global tensions for over forty years, had ended.

Bush dealt with his full share of international crises during his presidency: in China, in Latin America, and in the Middle East. He went to war briefly against Iraq, which had invaded Kuwait on August 2, 1990, with 120,000 troops and 850 tanks, due to a dispute over the oil-rich lands on the border between the two countries. The rest of the world had to decide whether to ignore this transgression and let the Arab nations settle their problems between themselves or, with the power of their collective outrage, to tell Iraq to get back across its borders where it belonged and quit bullying its neighbor. Bush and nations across the world immediately began taking every step short of war to force Iraq to behave:

1. The United States and Britain issued a joint condemnation of Iraq's aggression. (President Bush and Prime Minister Margaret Thatcher happened to be meeting together on the day of the invasion.)
2. The United States and Russia also issued a joint condemnation of the invasion, the first time since World War II that these two countries had cooperated on any issue. For the past forty years, they had almost automatically taken opposite sides of international disputes. No longer could other countries disputing with the United States depend on the Soviet Union to support them. This breakthrough was a high point in what the president called the toughest week in his life.
3. Bush called on the telephone the heads of state of many countries and asked for their support. And many of those countries joined in a coalition of money and armed forces to persuade Iraq that it should retreat. The president called this joining of powers "the new world order," in which law-abiding nations would insist that rogue nations honor others' boundaries.
4. The United States and the United Nations announced economic sanctions against Iraq.

President Bush meets with the emir of Kuwait, Jaber al-Ahmad al-Jaber al-Sabah, in the Oval Office to discuss Iraq's invasion of Kuwait, September 1990. Courtesy of George H. W. Bush Presidential Library and Museum.

5. The president asked the advice of other Middle Eastern leaders in Egypt, Saudi Arabia, and Jordan.
6. Bush ordered American warships to stand by in the Persian Gulf and sent armed forces to Saudi Arabia, a country also afraid of being invaded by Iraq. He called this Operation Desert Shield.
7. By November, the president was convinced that Iraq was not going to withdraw from Kuwait regardless of

pressure from other countries. He sent Secretary of State James Baker to Switzerland to meet with Iraq's foreign minister, to no avail.

8. Finally, Bush asked Congress to authorize military action, which it did by a narrow margin.
9. The United Nations gave Iraq until January 15 to pull out of Kuwait. Barbara Bush described this period as "tense . . . as if the whole world was holding its breath."

Believing they had run out of peaceful options, on January 17, coalition forces began making air strikes against the Iraqis. The Iraq War (also called the Persian Gulf War or Desert Storm) had begun. Air attacks peppered Iraqi military installations for thirty-eight days. On February 24, the ground assault began, and the enfeebled Iraqi army fled. After only four days, what has come to be known as the 100-Hour War ended in Iraq's defeat. American deaths numbered about three hundred; Iraqi deaths, eight to ten thousand. The Iraqi army, the fourth largest in the world, had been routed. This time, Bush did allow himself and all Americans to revel in their victory. He addressed a joint session of Congress in which every member of the audience waved small American flags in celebration.

Now Bush addressed another critical question. Should he pursue the Iraqis all the way to Baghdad, occupy the capital, and capture or kill President Saddam Hussein? He chose not to do that. He had achieved the goal of getting Iraq out of Kuwait, and he knew that more fighting would mean more American deaths and that once in the country, the US would spend millions of dollars and have difficulty getting

President Bush greets troops in Saudi Arabia during the Gulf War, November 1990. Courtesy of George H. W. Bush Presidential Library and Museum.

out again. A few criticized Bush for this decision, stating he was not being strong and triumphant and not finishing the job, but most Americans were elated with the victory and satisfied that he had made the right choice. They gave him an 89 percent approval rating, the highest any president had ever received. It looked as if George Bush would be a shoo-in for a second term, but economic difficulties at home loomed.

The president next turned his attention to the problems at home. During his tenure, two domestic bills passed that he was especially proud of, and a budget crisis proved intractable.

The Americans with Disabilities Act benefited some 43 million disabled Americans. It was the first legislation in the world to state that people with disabilities could not be discriminated against when they applied for jobs and that public transportation and public buildings (including hotels, restaurants, museums, and libraries) must be accessible to disabled users. Because of this act, we now commonly see curb and building ramps that can accommodate wheelchairs, buses that can be lowered for wheelchair access, braille signage in elevators, and sign-language interpreters at events. Before the passage of the Americans with Disabilities Act, most Americans were simply unaware how limited the lives of disabled citizens were, those who could not step off a curb or use an elevator or understand the words at a city council meeting.

When Bush signed the bill before two thousand guests, he was so touched by the courage of those who live with disabilities that he wrote to a friend afterward, "As I looked out at the audience . . . I was saying to myself 'don't choke up—hang in there.'" After the signing, Bush received a letter of appreciation from a woman who told him that her lawyer husband, in a wheelchair, had been turned down for thirty-nine jobs because of his disability. Bush named this man chairman of the Equal Employment Opportunity Commission.

Although it's easy to take the positive impact of this civil rights legislation for granted today, at the time, Bush and Congress received criticism from some who charged that structural changes to buildings and sidewalks would prove overly expensive and that bureaucracy to manage the changes would be cumbersome. This, however, was what the president had meant when he said as a candidate, "I want a kinder and gentler nation."

Another bill that critics called too expensive to be affordable was the Clean Air Amendments. Bush, however, re-

Flanked by supporters, President Bush signs the Americans with Disabilities Act, a landmark law preventing discrimination against people with disabilities, July 1990. Courtesy of George H. W. Bush Presidential Library and Museum.

mained deeply committed to conservation of the environment. He proposed provisions to reduce urban smog, lessen acid rain, and eliminate industrial emission of toxic chemicals. This bill passed easily.

Perhaps Bush's biggest domestic challenge was the economy and the budget. When he took office, he soon learned that the savings and loan industry was failing, and he felt compelled to spend more than $100 billion to save it, lest millions of Americans lose their mortgages on their houses or their money put in savings. The economy began to falter in other ways; unemployment rose to 7.8 percent, and inflation made people's money worth less. When it came time to write a budget, the government was already spending more money than it was taking in and suffering from a federal deficit of $2.8 trillion, which was inherited from the previous administration.

In spite of this deficit, Bush believed that his administration had spent money wisely on major issues like bailing out the savings and loan industry, guaranteeing civil rights for disabled Americans, and protecting the environment, but now the time had come to get the budget under control and erase the deficit, possible only if the government cut spending in as many areas as possible *and* raised taxes. This decision did not come easily to him because he, too, remembered his promise during the campaign when he had said, "Read my lips: no new taxes." He knew that those whose programs were cut and those whose taxes were raised, both Republicans and Democrats, would be furious. When he signed the bill, Richard Darman, his director of the Office of Management and Budget, remembered, "We all appreciated that he knew very well that he was taking an enormous personal risk—and that, unlike most conventional politicians, he was willing to sacrifice his own political interest for what he took to be the public good."

CHAPTER 6

LIFE IN THE WHITE HOUSE

By the time the Bushes reached the White House, their at-home family was reduced to Barbara, George, and their springer spaniel Millie, but Millie soon added to their numbers by having six puppies. One—Ranger—so endeared himself to the president that they kept him, and the two dogs slept with the Bushes at night. Ranger woke the president and First Lady each morning at five o'clock, and the two dogs kept their owners company while they read the newspapers and drank coffee in bed. Millie was so popular with the public that she received an average of a hundred thousand letters a year. Ranger was a favorite with the staff, so much so that the president had to send a memo around asking the employees not to feed the dog treats because he was gaining too much weight.

The First Lady focused much of her activity on literacy after she learned that a substantial number of both adults and children read poorly, if at all. She read to children at schools and on the radio weekly and established the Barbara Bush Foundation for Family Literacy.

She remained active physically by swimming every day, playing tennis several times a week, and tossing horseshoes with her husband and the staff. She liked having the children and grandchildren visit the White House regularly, saying it made their life in this rarefied atmosphere feel more normal.

She had her share of traveling to do and speeches to make. At first, she wanted to fly commercially, but the Secret Service would not allow her to. They reminded her that her presence on a commercial flight would delay takeoff while they checked the luggage—and other passengers—for possible threats against Barbara's life.

One speech she found particularly trying. When she addressed the graduating class at Wellesley, a women's college in Massachusetts, a group of 150 seniors protested because she was a stay-at-home woman rather than a career woman. Tension filled the air when she began her talk, but she won the audience over when she said, "And who knows? Somewhere out in this audience may even be someone who will one day follow in my footsteps, and preside over the White House as the president's spouse—and I wish him well."

Fortunately, the president relished entertaining because parties occupied large chunks of their time. In their first one hundred days, the White House was the site for eighteen receptions, sixteen dinners, twenty-four coffees or teas, nineteen lunches, two breakfasts, and fifty-one overnight guests. In four years, the Bushes entertained thirty-two heads of state at elaborate state dinners with hundreds of guests wearing long gowns and formal suits.

Parties tested the White House staff's ability to deal with the unexpected. At one, honoring Lech Walesa of Poland, a guest backed up to the dining table and leaned on it; the table broke in the middle, tumbling food, flowers, and the candelabra to the floor. A ready staff ushered guests to a nearby room while the group scrambled to put the table back together and clean up the spilled food.

If the Bushes were not entertaining at the White House, they often were showing foreign guests American culture. President Bush took the president of Egypt to a Baltimore Orioles game, the Israeli prime minister to the Smithsonian's Air and Space Museum, and the king of Jordan to George Washington's home at Mount Vernon.

When an official event was not planned, the president and Mrs. Bush liked to have friends over for dinner and to watch a movie in their private theater and then walk their dogs before going to bed. Once, late at night, they were strolling the grounds and went over to talk to two women tourists they saw on the sidewalk outside the fence. The women said their families would not believe that they had actually met President and Mrs. Bush, so Barbara went back inside the house and wrote both of the women's families that night to say it was true. Several weeks later, one of the tourists, a cosmetician at a People's Drug Store in Maryland, made a contribution to the White House Endowment Fund, which helps refurbish the state rooms at the residence, in appreciation for the president and First Lady's exceptional courtesy.

The White House staff planned all occasions with imagination and attention to detail, but never more so than at Christmas. On the Bushes' first Christmas, the theme for the tree—storybook characters—was decided in February, and craftsmen made decorations for almost the entire year. By December, a grouping of beautiful Christmas trees stood at the entrance to the White House, and the main tree, placed

President and Mrs. Bush with their grandchildren at Camp David, Thurmont, Maryland, September 1992. Courtesy of George H. W. Bush Presidential Library and Museum.

in the Blue Room, arrived on a horse-drawn wagon and was soon covered with the eighty handmade storybook figures. A few days later, President and Mrs. Bush came home to find that a fourteen-foot tree covered with their family's decorations and gingerbread cookies had also appeared in their private quarters. For two weeks before Christmas, choirs from all over the country took turns singing carols, and the Bushes invited many groups and tours to enjoy the decorations with them. About Christmas, Barbara Bush said, "All our children came home. Their in-laws were marvelous about letting us have them every year George was president. I think that they knew that George needed them. He needed their support, their jokes, and their love."

Soon after becoming First Lady, Barbara Bush began suffering from eye trouble and exhaustion, making her busy schedule even more difficult. Doctors diagnosed her with Graves' disease, a thyroid disorder caused by a malfunctioning autoimmune system. Surprisingly, before long, President Bush received the same diagnosis. Then, against all odds, Millie the dog was diagnosed with another autoimmune disease, lupus. Puzzled, experts searched the vice president's house, trying to discover if some abnormality, perhaps in the air or water, had made three members of the same household ill with similar diseases before they got to the White House. They found nothing, but son George W., often the comedian in the family, called to suggest that if his parents would quit drinking out of Millie's water bowl, they would not be sick.

The news media reported even the smallest likes and dislikes of the first family. When George Bush asked the White House kitchen not to serve him broccoli because he didn't like it and had been forced to eat it as a child, the press announced the news to the entire country. Broccoli growers sent a truckload of broccoli to the Bushes, and many people mailed in recipes for ways they thought the president would like broccoli. The whole country talked about broccoli, but the president remained adamant. "I felt strongly," he said. "I liberated many four-, five-, six-year-old kids all across this country who shared my hate for broccoli."

1992 was an election year. George Bush faced two opponents: the Democratic governor of Arkansas, Bill Clinton, and a billionaire businessman from Texas, Ross Perot. Even though the president had deftly ushered the nation through the end of the Cold War with Russia and had brought the Gulf War with Iraq to a quick and successful conclusion, the public was focused not on foreign affairs, but on the economy at home. A recession and high unemployment unsettled them. Voters could not forget that George Bush had said "No new taxes" in the previous election but then raised taxes after he became president. Bill Clinton charmed voters with a personable, optimistic style. Ross Perot's entry into the race took votes away from George Bush. The final count was 43 percent for Clinton, 37 percent for Bush, and 19 percent for Perot. Sixty-three percent of voters had rejected President Bush, who was deeply hurt by the results.

Another pain, greater than that of defeat, struck the president two weeks after the election when his ninety-one-year-old mother died following a stroke. During her last hours, the president sat beside her hospital bed, sobbing and holding her hand. He discovered on her bedside table letters he had written to her when he was a boy at boarding school and a birthday card he had sent her when he was eighteen years old. The woman who had probably been one of the greatest influences on his life was gone.

CHAPTER 7
RETIREMENT

George and Barbara Bush began their last day in the White House sharing memories as they walked across the grounds hand in hand, their dogs alongside chasing squirrels. Their children began calling early to check that they were all right. They said a tearful goodbye to the White House staff. President Bush sat at his desk in the Oval Office one last time, leaving a gracious note on the desktop for Bill Clinton, telling him that he would be "rooting hard" for him. Then President-elect Clinton, Vice President–elect Al Gore, and their spouses arrived, and the couples set out together for Clinton's inauguration at the Capitol.

Finally, the time had come to leave Washington. The Bushes had grown up in New England, spent eighteen years of their early married life in Texas, and lived twenty-six years in Washington, DC, with short stints to other places. When it came time to retire, George Bush said, "we never thought twice about what to do next: go home to Texas, of course." (In addition, they became New Englanders again in Kennebunkport for a large chunk of the year.)

Vice President and Mrs. Quayle accompanied the Bushes to Andrews Air Force Base, where a plane awaited. Friends and family flew with the Bushes to Houston, creating for them a lighthearted atmosphere on this solemn day. Many of the guests on the plane turned around and returned to Washington as soon as they saw President and Mrs. Bush safely home to Texas.

Surprises awaited the Bushes. Everywhere they looked, yellow ribbons and people holding "Welcome Home" signs greeted them. Flowers from their new neighbors filled their rental house. The next morning they woke up at five thirty, but no staff appeared to serve them coffee. They made their own bed, walked, and fed their dogs, and started a new chapter in their lives, one in which Barbara cooked while George filled the dishwasher.

First came the building of the George H. W. Bush Presidential Library and Museum and the adjoining Bush School of Government and Public Service on a ninety-acre plot at Texas A&M University in College Station. The center houses forty-four million documents associated with the former president's career, exhibits that tell his life story, and an apartment for the Bushes' use. On the grounds is a pond in which the public can fish and a statue entitled *The Day the Wall Came Down*, depicting the end of the Cold War in the form of stallions jumping over the demolished Berlin Wall.

The Bushes decided they would be buried on this site. They moved their daughter Robin's grave from Connecticut so she could lie beside them and instructed that, when the time came, there be no monuments—only white crosses as grave markers.

Bush became a part of the Houston community again by serving on the advisory board for MD Anderson Cancer Center and raising millions of dollars for nonprofits both in

Houston and nationally. He accepted paid speaking engagements, which he called "pay the rent" speeches. He participated in the physical activities he thrived on: tennis, golf, horseshoes, quail hunting, fishing, and driving his boat.

The Bushes traveled frequently, including nine times to China. One trip particularly stands out, a return to the spot where his plane had been shot down in the Pacific fifty-eight years before. Here he placed floral wreaths in the water in memory of his two lost crewmen, about whom he had thought many times in the intervening years.

Most satisfying was sinking back into family life. "Now that my political days are over," he said, "I can honestly say that the three most rewarding titles bestowed upon me are the three that I've got left—a husband, a father, and a granddad." In retirement, family could take precedence, and the family was large: five children, seventeen grandchildren, and eight great-grandchildren.

From time to time, the current president would call on him to serve the country. More than once, former Presidents Bush and Clinton worked together to help with crises. The two raised funds for Asian tsunami victims in 2004, for Hurricane Katrina relief a year later, and then for Hurricane Ike in 2008. In the process, the two—at ages that could make them father and son—became friends.

The Bushes participated vicariously as they watched two of their sons rise in politics. Jeb became governor of Florida and George governor of Texas. When asked if she and the former president were dismayed at two of their children's choosing the arduous world of politics, Barbara Bush answered, "No, it made us think, as parents, that we must have done something right." In 2000, just twelve years after his fa-

Only the second father and son to hold the presidency, former President George H. W. Bush, the forty-first president, poses with President George W. Bush, the forty-third president, at Camp David, Thurmont, Maryland, December 2001. Courtesy of George W. Bush Presidential Library.

ther had been elected the forty-first president of the United States, George W. Bush became the forty-third. Not since John Quincy Adams followed John Adams to the same office, 175 years earlier, had a father and son both ascended to the presidency.

During his sons' political campaigns, the former president quietly worked to raise money but never stepped out front to make speeches, and although the two Presidents Bush spoke on the telephone frequently, they and those around them say they did not discuss presidential affairs but spent most of their conversations on family. When asked how he kept from second-guessing his son's decisions as president, the senior

Bush said that he couldn't because he did not have all the information a president had with which to decide. In addition to being immensely proud of his son's being the president, George H. W. Bush also suffered as he witnessed the inevitable criticism from the press and the public that any president endures, even if the critics did not have all the information. "Watching your son take a pounding from his critics," he said, was much harder than taking one yourself.

Honors came the former president's way, including having the international airport in Houston and an aircraft carrier named for him, and being presented with the Medal of Freedom, the highest civilian award in the United States. At the awards ceremony in the White House, President Obama said, "His life is a testament that public service is a noble calling." The Lyndon B. Johnson Foundation presented him with the LBJ Liberty and Justice for All Award, which the chairman of the LBJ Foundation said "recognizes his demonstrated qualities of civility and bipartisanship in public service."

The former president found time to write, but he did not publish a memoir as many presidents have because, as he said, "I don't want to direct history." He did collect a lifetime of letters he had written and put them in book form, and he collaborated with his former national security adviser Brent Scowcroft on a book about foreign policy.

When he was eighty-nine, he returned to the White House, at President Obama's invitation, to present an award. In the first year of his presidency, he and Barbara had begun the Points of Light Foundation, and for twenty-three years they had presented a Daily Point of Light Award to a volunteer who had "sparked change and improved the world"—people

President Bush called "the soul of America." On that day the honor went to recipients of the five thousandth award—Floyd Hammer and Kathy Hamilton of Union, Iowa—who, through their own efforts, were distributing free meals to hungry children in fifteen nations and the United States. A beaming George Bush watched the ceremony from his wheelchair, sporting his signature loud socks, which on this day were unmatching and featured red and white stripes.

As he grew older, George Bush, still full of spunk, realized he had unfinished business. The memory of having to desert his flaming plane in World War II prompted him to plan a parachute jump for his seventy-fifth birthday. He remembered his fear on that day fifty-five years earlier—hitting his head on the tail of the plane as he exited, pulling the cord too soon, plunging into the depths of the ocean before surfacing, and then outrunning the enemy while crying and vomiting. He wanted to do it again—this time correctly, and as a pleasure, not a horror.

With help from the US Army, he jumped solo on his seventy-fifth birthday over the lawn of the Bush Library in College Station, free-falling at one hundred miles an hour, then floating happily to the ground. He was to repeat these jumps on his eightieth, eighty-fifth, and ninetieth birthdays.

On his eightieth—again at the library—the Army decided the wind was too unpredictable and had him harnessed to another parachuter. When he landed, he skidded on his backside the last few yards but proclaimed it "a day of wonder . . . for the old guy." One of his birthday guests, former Soviet leader Mikhail Gorbachev, said the president had pestered him for two years to jump beside him but he had declined.

President and Mrs. Bush with a member of the Golden Knights shortly after Bush went skydiving to celebrate his eighty-fifth birthday, Kennebunkport, Maine, June 2009. Courtesy of George H. W. Bush Presidential Library and Museum and the US Army Golden Knights Parachute Team.

By his eighty-fifth birthday, the president was walking with a cane. This time he jumped near the family's vacation home in Kennebunkport, harnessed to a member of the Army's team of retired parachuters, the Golden Knights. He said afterward, "It's a great, exhilarating feeling. I don't feel a day over eighty-four."

By his ninetieth birthday, he was spending most of his time in a wheelchair, but he still made the jump—again in Kennebunkport but this time from a helicopter because he could exit it more easily. He jumped with the same veterans' group as before, harnessed again to the man who had accompanied him on his eighty-fifth, Sergeant First Class Mike Elliott. When their red-white-and-blue parachute brought them to earth, men picked him up and helped him back into his wheelchair, and he received a welcome-back kiss from Barbara, who was waiting on the lawn.

In an interview, he discounted the accomplishment and praised Sergeant Elliott. "You're in the arms of a great big, strong guy," he said. "He does all the work . . . and then as you land, he says, 'Pick up your feet,' . . . and I'm in his arms and my feet up, and he lands with his feet down on the ground . . . there's no jarring."

Bush's parachute jump on his ninetieth birthday served as a fitting celebration for a man who had always participated wholeheartedly and with determination, who appreciated the accomplishment of others as much as his own, and who wanted nothing more at the end of the day than to return home to Barbara.

On April 17, 2018, Bush lost his wife of seventy-three years. After facing a series of health issues, Barbara died of heart failure at age ninety-two. Bush expressed his grief in a statement in which he said, "I always thought of Barbara as the most loving and gracious woman I have ever known. . . . She was, in every sense, a great lady. And we are all better for having known her."

Bush's health was also declining. The man who had championed the Americans with Disabilities Act had been using a wheelchair for the last several years of his life due to a form of Parkinson's disease. Grieving from Barbara's passing, he lived to see his ninety-fourth birthday in June before his own death from complications related to Parkinson's and a blood infection in their Houston home on November 30, 2018.

The country mourned Bush as a man of great character—one of decency, humility, and dedication to public service. In his eulogy for his father, George W. Bush called him a "great and good man." Choked up with emotion, he said, "Through our tears, let us see the blessings of knowing and loving you—a great and noble man, and the best father a son or daughter could have."

ACKNOWLEDGMENTS

After the pleasure of writing, preparing for publication seems more like a chore unless you have the added pleasure, as I did, of working with people who are collegial, efficient, and knowledgeable. Thank you to David B. Jones, chief executive officer of the George Bush Presidential Library Foundation, and to members of his staff Mary Finch, Sarah Lawrence, and Amanda Nedbalek. Thank you to Jean Becker, chief of staff for President George H. W. Bush. Thank you to Holly Z. Taylor, editor and head of publications at the Dolph Briscoe Center for American History in Austin. And thank you always to Mark Updegrove, to whom I often turn for advice.

SELECTED BIBLIOGRAPHY

Bush, Barbara. *A Memoir.* Charles Scribner's Sons, 1994.

Bush, George. *All The Best: My Life in Letters and Other Writings.* Simon & Schuster, 1999.

Koch, Doro Bush. *My Father, My President.* Warner Books, 2006.

Naftali, Timothy. *George H. W. Bush.* Henry Holt and Company, 2007.

Parmet, Herbert S. *George Bush: The Life of a Lone Star Yankee.* Scribner, 1997.

Updegrove, Mark K. *Second Acts: Presidential Lives and Legacies After the White House.* Lyons Press, 2006.

Wicker, Tom. *George Herbert Walker Bush.* Viking Book, 2004.

www.ingramcontent.com/pod-product-compliance
Lightning Source LLC
Jackson TN
JSHW021256100426
100637JS00002B/9

* 9 7 8 1 4 7 7 3 3 2 1 7 7 *